100+ Frequently Asked Interview Q & A

in *Swift Programming*

By Bandana Ojha

1

Introduction

Frequently Asked Interview Q & A in Swift Programming book contains 100+ questions and answers and we assure that you will get 90% frequently asked interview questions in Swift programming. This book will clear your fundamentals, concepts and boost your confidence to appear any iOS development interview in any companies anywhere in the world whether it is telephonic or face to face.

Wishing good luck to all our readers!!!

Check out our other interview Q & A series. Like Interview Questions & Answers in Manual Testing, Selenium Testing, Mobile Testing, Core Java programming, Advance Java programming, J2EE programming, Python programming , Scala programming and iOS development.

1. What are generics in swift and what problem do they solve?

Generics are used to make algorithms safely work with types. In Swift, generics can be used both in functions and data types, e.g. in classes, structures or enumerations.

Generics solve the problem of code duplication. A common case is when you have a method that takes a type of parameter and you must duplicate it just to accommodate a parameter of another type.

2. What is Swift - Access Control?

To restrict the access to code blocks, modules and abstraction it is done through access control. Classes, structures and enumerations can be accessed according to their properties, methods, initializers and subscripts by the usage of access control mechanisms. Constants, variables and the functions in a protocol are restricted and allowed to access as global and local through access control. Access control applied to properties, types and functions can be referred as 'entities'.

3. How to define variables and constant in Swift?

Constants and variables must be declared before they are used. You declare constants with the let keyword and variables with the var keyword.

let maximumnumberofstudentsintheclass= 100

var totalstudentpresentintheclass = 50

4. What is an optional in Swift and How it helps?

An optional is used to let a variable of any type represent the lack of value. In Objective-C, the absence of value is available in reference types only, and it uses the nil special value. Value types, such as int or float, do not have such ability.

Swift extends the lack of value concept to both reference and value types with optional. An optional variable can hold either a value or nil any time.

5. How can you make a property optional in Swift?

Declaring a question mark "?" in the code can make a property optional.

If a property doesn't hold a value, then this symbol "?" helps in avoiding the runtime errors.

6. What is NSZombie?

It's a memory debugging aid. Specifically, when you set NSZombieEnabled then whenever an object reaches retain count 0, rather than begin deallocated it morphs itself into an NSZombie instance. Whenever such a zombie receives a message, it logs a warning rather than crashing or behaving in an unpredictable way.

7. Explain what Lazy stored properties is and when it is useful?

Lazy stored properties are used for a property whose initial values is not calculated until the first time it is used. You can declare a lazy stored property by writing the lazy modifier before its declaration. Lazy properties are useful when the initial value for a property is reliant on outside factors whose values are unknown.

8. In Swift enumerations, what's the difference between raw values and associated values?

Raw values are used to associate constant (literal) values to enum cases. The value type is part of the enum type, and each enum case must specify a unique raw value (duplicate values are not allowed).

Associated values are used to associate arbitrary data to a specific enum case. Each enum case can have zero or more associated values, declared as a tuple in the case definition

9. What is de-initializer and how it is written in Swift?

A de-initializer is declared immediately before a class instance is de-allocated. You write de-initializer with the deinit keyword. De-initializer is written without any parenthesis, and it does not take any parameters. It is written as

deinit {

// perform the deinitialization

}

10. What is Swift - Protocol?

Protocols provide us with a blueprint for the Methods, properties and other requirements functionality. They are just described as the methods or properties skeleton instead of the implementation. Methods and properties implementation can also further be done by defining classes, functions and enumerations. Conformance of the protocol is now defined as the methods or properties satisfying the requirements of the protocol.

11. What is Initialization ?

Initialization is the process of preparing an instance of a class, structure, or enumeration for use. This process involves setting an initial value for each stored property on that instance and performing any other setup or initialization that is required before the new instance is ready for use.

You implement this initialization process by defining initializers, which are like special methods that can be called to create a new instance of a particular type. Unlike Objective-C initializers, Swift initializers do not return a value. Their primary role is to ensure that new instances of a type are correctly initialized before they are used for the first time.

12. What are Initializers ?

Initializers are called to create a new instance of a particular type. In its simplest form, an initializer is like an instance method with no parameters, written using the init keyword:

```
init() {

// perform some initialization here

}
```

13. What is the characteristics of Switch in Swift?

It supports any kind of data, and not only synchronize but also checks for equality

When a case is matched in switch, the program exists from the switch case and does not continue checking next cases. So, you don't need to explicitly break out the switch at the end of case

Switch statement must be exhaustive, which means that you must cover all possible values for your variable

There is no fall through in switch statements and therefore break is not required

14. Explain what is optional chaining?

Optional chaining is a process of querying and calling properties. Multiple queries can be chained together, and if any link in the chain is nil then, the entire chain fails.

15. Why do we use availability attributes ?

Apple wants to support one system version back, meaning that we should support iOS9 or iOS8. Availability Attributes lets us to support previous version iOS.

16. What are the collection types available in Swift?

Swift Programming Language provides three main collection types called Arrays, Sets and Dictionaries. These three collections are used to store a collection of values. Dictionaries are not ordered collections which will have key-value pairs associations. These three data types are always clear about the types of values and keys associated with them. The different or wrong type key or values cannot be inserted into these collection types. This leads to less error-prone or types checking safety at runtime. The collection types Arrays, Sets, and Dictionaries are mutable. This means that the values can be changed and modified as per the requirement or the operations need to be done.

17. What is a guard statement in Swift?

The main use of guard statement is to transfer program control out of a scope on certain conditions. These statements are similar with if statements which executes statements based on certain condition (Boolean value) but unlike if, the guard statements only run when certain conditions are not met.

Moreover, statements inside the guard must exit from the scope. Therefore, we have to user program control statements return, break, continue or throw at the end of the guard statement.

18. What are tuples in Swift?

Tuple is a group of different values represented as one . According to apple, a tuple type is a comma-separated list of zero or more types, enclosed in parentheses.

19. What is the question mark ? in Swift?

The question mark ? is used during the declaration of a property, as it tells the compiler that this property is optional. The property may hold a value or not, in the latter case it's possible to avoid runtime errors when accessing that property by using ?.

20. *What is the difference between Swift and 'Objective-C' language?*

In swift,

-The variable and constants are declared before their use

-You must use "let" keyword for constant and "var" keyword for variable

-There is no need to end code with semi-colon

-Concatenating strings is easy in swift and allows to make a new string from a mix of constants, literals, variables, as well as expressions

-Swift does not require to create a separate interface like Objective C. You can define classes in a single file (.swift)

-Swift enables you to define methods in class, structure or enumeration

-You use " +=" Operator to add an item

In objective C,

-You must declare variable as NSString and constant as int

- Variable is declared as " and constant as "

-The code ends with semi-colon

-You must choose between NSMutableString and NSString for string to be modified.

21. *What is Memento Pattern ?*

Memento Pattern is effectively employed within the iOS application platform framework. It plays a vital role in saving your stuff somewhere.

And then, the externalized state can never be taken back else it becomes the violating encapsulation. All the private personal information will be transferred safety.

One of Apple's specialized implementations of the Memento pattern is Archiving other hand iOS uses the Memento pattern as part of State Restoration.

22. What is Observer Pattern ?

Observer pattern is one among the internal functioning aspect of iOS application platform. In the Observer pattern, one object notifies other objects of any state changes.

23. What is Facade Design Pattern?

The Facade design pattern furnishes the best known for providing a single interface to a complex subsystem. With the aid of Facade Design Pattern, In spite of using an user to a group of classes with their APIs, you only compose one simple unified API.

24. What is Singleton Pattern?

The Singleton design pattern ensures that only one instance exists for a given class and that there's a global access point to that instance. It usually uses lazy loading to create the single instance when it's needed the first time.

25. What is an Adapter?

It lets the classes with incompatible interfaces to work together and it wraps itself around the object to expose a standard interface to interact with that object.

26. Explain Regular expression and Responder chain?

Regular Expression – These are the special string patterns that describe how a search is performed through a string.

Responder Chain – It is a hierarchy of objects that obtain the opportunity to respond to the events.

27. What is core data ?

Core data is an object graph manager which also can persist object graphs to the persistent store on a disk. An object graph is like a map of all the different model objects in a typical model view controller iOS application.

28. Differentiate the concepts of retain and copy?

Retaining in the sense relates to the aspect in which the total count increases by one. This states that the instance of the object will be kept in memory unless it retains count totally drops to the value of null or zero.

Whereas, the term Copy indicates that the object will be cloned with duplicate values.

29. How multiple line comment can be written in swift?

Multiple line comment can be written as forward-slash followed by an asterisk (/*) and end with an asterisk followed by a forward slash (*/).

30. What's the difference between Any and AnyObject?

AnyObject refers to any instance of a class, and is equivalent to id in Objective-C. It's useful when you specifically want to work with a reference type, because it won't allow any of Swift's structs or enums to be used. AnyObject is also used when you want to restrict a protocol so that it can be used only with classes.

Any refers to any instance of a class, struct, or enum – literally anything at all.

31. What are the differences between functions and methods in Swift?

Functions in Swift are defined as a self-contained code that performs a task as per the requirement. The function will be identified by its name to call whenever that task is needed. To declare a function, func will be used. A function can be called by calling its name with a list of parameters or arguments to be passed in the parenthesis of function.

Methods are functions that are associated with a particular type. Classes, structures, and enumerations can all define instance methods, which encapsulate specific tasks and functionality for working with an instance of a given type.

32. What is Swift Programming?

Swift is a powerful, open-source, safe, multi-paradigm and compiled programming language designed and developed by Apple Inc. It is a safe, fast and interactive programming language for iOS, macOS, watchOS, tvOS and Linux.

33. Is Swift an object-oriented language or a functional language?

Swift is a hybrid language that supports both paradigms. It implements the three fundamental principles of OOP: Encapsulation Inheritance Polymorphism as for Swift being a functional language, there are different but equivalent ways to define it.

34. What are the advantages of Swift?

Swift is safe

Swift is fast

Swift is open source

Swift is approachable

Swift is easy to learn

35. How many ways to pass data in Swift ?

There are many ways such as Delegate, KVO, Segue, and NSNotification, Target-Action, Callbacks.

36. What is the meaning of id ?

id is a pointer to any type, it always points to an Objective-C object. The AnyObject protocol is similar and it helps bridge the gap between Swift and Objective-C.

37. Differentiate #import, #include and @class?

#import: Improved version of include, brings entire header file into current file

#include: With objective C, there is performance hit with #include, compiler must open each header file to notice the include guard.

@class: A forward declaration compiler directive, It tells the compiler that class exists, does not know anything about class. It minimizes the amount of code seen by the compiler or linker.

38. List the features of Swift Programming?

Below are the features of swift programming -

Variables are always initialized before use.

Memory is managed automatically.

Arrays and integers are checked for overflow.

Switch function can be used instead of using "if" statement.

It eliminates the classes that are in unsafe mode.

39. What are new features in Swift 4.0?

New features in swift 4.0 are

-Faster, easier to use Strings that retain Unicode correctness

-Smart key paths for type-safe, efficient, extensible key value coding for Swift types

-Added some enhancements to creating dictionary and Set types

-Extends to supports of serialization to Struct

-Tuples and multiple return values

-Structs that support methods, extensions, and protocols

-Native error handling using try/catch/throw

40. What are the control transfer statements in swift?

The control transfer statements in swift are:

Continue

Break

Fallthrough

Return

41. How do you handle async tasks?

Asynchronous programming is a vital part of any iOS application. Networking, local storage, and other heavy computation tasks should be handled in the background to avoid blocking UI and having users wait or system kill your application.

42. How should one handle errors in Swift?

In Swift, it's possible to declare that a function throws an error. It is, therefore, the caller's responsibility to handle the error or propagate it. This is like how Java handles the situation.

You simply declare that a function can throw an error by appending the throws keyword to the function name. Any function that calls such a method must call it from a try block.

43. Explain Priority Inversion and Priority Inheritance.

If high priority thread waits for low priority thread, this is called Priority Inversion. if low priority thread temporarily inherits the priority of the highest priority thread, this is called Priority Inheritance.

44. Explain Sequence in Swift.

Sequence is a basic type in Swift for defining an aggregation of elements that distribute sequentially in a row. All collection types are inherited from Sequence such as Array, Set, Dictionary.

45. What is @objc inference?

You can tag a Swift declaration with @objc to indicate that it should be available to Objective-C. In Swift 3 many declarations were automatically inferred to be made available to Objective-C. The most common place for this is any Swift method we want to refer to using a selector.

46. What is type inference?

Swift uses type inference to work out the appropriate type. Type inference enables a compiler to deduce the type of a particular expression automatically when it compiles your code, simply by examining the values you provide.

47. Explain Encoding, Decoding , Serialization and Deserialization in Swift.

Serialization is the process of converting data into a single string or json, so it can be stored or transmitted easily. Serialization, also known as encoding. The reverse process of turning a single string into a data is called decoding, or deserialization.

48. What is Codable?

Codable is a protocol that a type can conform to, to declare that it can be encoded and decoded. It's basically an alias for the Encodable and Decodable protocols.

There are many types in Swift which are codable out of the box: Int, String, Date, Array and many other types from the Standard Library and the Foundation framework. If you want your type to be codable, the simplest way to do it is by conforming to Codable and making sure all its stored properties are also codable.

49. Explain some common execution states in iOS?

The states of the common execution can be as follows:

Not running – This state means that there is no code that is being executed and the application is completely switched off.

Inactive – This state means that the application is running in the background and is not receiving any events.

Active – This state means that the applications are running in the background and is receiving the events.

Background – This state means that the application is executing the code in the background.

Suspended – This state means that the application is in the background and is not executing.

50. What is a function in swift?

A function is a group of statements that defines an action to be performed. The main use of a function is to make the code reusable.

51. Name types of functions in swift?

Depending on whether a function is predefined or created by programmer; there are two types of function:

Library functions - Functions that are defined already in Swift Framework.

User-defined functions - Functions created by the programmer themselves.

52. What is a category (ObjC) or Extension (Swift) and when is it used?

A category is a way of adding additional methods to a class without extending it. It is often used to add a collection of related methods. A common use case is to add additional methods to build in classes in the Cocoa frameworks. For example, adding async download methods to the UIImage class.

53. What's the difference between using a delegate and notification?

Both are used for sending values and messages to an interested party. A delegate is for one-to-one communication and is a pattern promoted by Apple. In delegation the class raising events will have a property for the delegate and will typically expect it to implement some protocol. The delegating class can then call the _delegate_s protocol methods. Notification allows a class to broadcast events across the entire application to any interested parties. The broadcasting class doesn't need to know anything about the listeners for this event, therefore notification is very useful in helping to decouple components in an application.

54. What is dictionary in swift?

It enables you to store the key-value pairs and access the value by providing the key. It is like a hash table in other programming language.

55. How to access dictionary elements in Swift?

As arrays, you can access elements of a dictionary by using subscript syntax. You need to include key of the value you want to access within square brackets immediately after the name of the dictionary.

56. How to modify dictionary elements in Swift?

You can add elements of in dictionary by using subscript syntax. You need to include new key as the subscript index and assign a new value of the type as of Dictionary.

57. In Swift, what is the difference between a struct and a class?

The main difference is; Structs are passed by value and classes are passed by reference.

58. What is the base class in Swift?

Swift classes do not inherit from a universal base class. Classes you define without specifying a superclass automatically become base classes for you to build upon

59. What is Xcode?

Xcode is Apple's integrated development environment (IDE) that you use to design apps for Apple products. It provides various tools to manage your entire development workflow from creating your app, to testing, submitting and optimizing it to the App store.

60. How to import Objective-C files into Swift?

To import a set of Objective-C files in the same app target as your Swift code, you rely on an Objective-C bridging header to expose those files to Swift. Xcode offers to create this header file when you add a Swift file to an existing Objective-C app, or an Objective-C file to an existing Swift app.

61. What is an Identifier in swift?

A Swift identifier is a name which is used to represent a variable, function, or any another user-defined item. An identifier begins with an alphabet A to Z or a to z or an underscore _ along with by zero or more letters, and digits (0 to 9), underscores.

Swift does not permit special characters like @, $, and % within the identifiers. Swift being a case sensitive programming language, Manpower and manpower are two separate identifiers in Swift.

62. What are literals?

A literal is a source code representation of a value of an integer, string type, or floating-point number, below are few examples of literals –

32   // Integer literal

6.9876   // Floating-point literal

"Hello Jack!" // String literal

63. What are the Tokens in Swift?

A Swift program contains different tokens and a token may be a keyword, an identifier, a string literal, a constant, or a symbol.

64. Why optional binding is used?

Optional binding is used to find out whether an optional contains a value, and if so, to make that value available as a temporary constant or variable.

An optional binding for the if statement is as stated below–

```
if let constantName = someOptional {

statements

}
```

65. What is Swift decision making?

Swift decision-making structures require that the developer will specify one or more conditions to be evaluated first or tested by the program, alongside with the statements to be executed if the condition is determined to be true, and optionally, other statements to be executed if the condition is determined to be false.

66. What is Swift - Loops?

Programming languages deliver several control structures which let user for more complicated execution paths.

A loop statement lets the user to run a statement or group of statements several multiple times.

67. What is Swift - Extensions?

Functionality of an already existing class, structure or enumeration type can be added with the help of the extensions. Type functionality can also be added with the extensions but overriding the functionality is not possible with extensions.

68. What is Swift - Optional Chaining?

The processing of querying, calling properties, subscripts and methods on the optional that may be 'nil' can be defined as optional chaining. Optional chaining return two values -

if optional contains a 'value' then calling its related property, methods and subscripts returns values.

if optional contains a 'nil' value all its its related property, methods and subscripts returns nil.

69. Explain any three-shift pattern matching techniques in swift.

Typecasting Patterns – This pattern allows you to match or cast the types.

Wildcard Patterns – This pattern matches as well as ignores any kind and type of value.

Optional Patterns – This pattern is used to match the optional values.

70. What is the use of exclamation mark !?

Exclamation mark "!" is used to tell the compiler that, this variable/constant contains a value and use it i.e. unwrap the optional.

71. Explain the difference between atomic and nonatomic synthesized properties?

Atomic and non-atomic refers to whether the setters/getters for a property will atomically read and write values to the property. When the atomic keyword is used on a property, any access to it will be "synchronized". Therefore, a call to the getter will be guaranteed to return a valid value, however this does come with a small performance penalty. Hence in some situations nonatomic is used to provide faster access to a property, but there is a chance of a race condition causing the property to be nil under rare circumstances (when a value is being set from another thread and the old value was released from memory, but the new value hasn't yet been fully assigned to the location in memory for the property).

72. Can you add a stored property by using an extension?

No, it's not possible. An extension can be used to add new behavior to an existing type, but not to alter the type itself or its interface. If you add a stored property, you'd need extra memory to store the new value. An extension cannot manage such a task.

73. What is the use of double question marks "?? " ?

To provide a default value for a variable.

    let missingName : String? = nil

    let realName : String? = "Keneilth"

    let existentName : String = missingName ?? realName

74. What is Sequence in Swift?

Sequence is a basic type in Swift for defining an aggregation of elements that distribute sequentially in a row. All collection types inherit from Sequence such as Array, Set, Dictionary.

75. *What is method swizzling?*

Method swizzling is the process of changing the implementation of an existing selector at runtime. Simply speaking, we can change the functionality of a method at runtime.

76. *How is memory management handled in Swift?*

Swift uses Automatic Reference Counting (ARC). ARC keeps track of strong references to instances of classes and increases or decreases their reference count accordingly when you assign or unassign instances of classes (reference types) to constants, properties, and variables. It deallocates memory used by objects whose reference count dropped to zero. ARC does not increase or decrease the reference count of value types because, when assigned, these are copied. By default, if you don't specify otherwise, all the references will be strong references.

77. Explain JSONEncoder and JSONDecoder in Swift4.

JSONEncoder :Encodable protocol to take instances of our object and turn it into data. With that data, we can store it to the files, send it to the server, whatever you need to do with it.

JSONDecoder :Decodable protocol, which allows us to take data and create instances of our object, populated with the data passed down from the server.

78. What is AutoLayout?

AutoLayout provides a flexible and powerful layout system that describes how views and the UI controls calculates the size and position in the hierarchy.

Auto Layout dynamically calculates the size and position of all the views in your view hierarchy, based on constraints placed on those views.

79. How can you write a multiple line command Swift?

The multiple line comment is written in between the symbols (/*) at the start and (*/) at the end.

80. What is the difference between SQL and SQLite?

SQL is query language. Sqlite is embeddable relational database management system. Unlike other databases (like SQL Server and MySQL) SQLite does not support stored procedures. SQLite is file-based, unlike other databases, like SQL Server and MySQL which are server-based.

81. Why code review should be done?

Code reviews is one of the most effective development methodologies. It helps understand the problem better, share knowledge, share techniques, catch bugs, share ownership of the codebase, etc.

82. What is type aliasing in swift?

A type alias allows you to provide a new name for an existing type into your program. After a type alias is declared, the aliased name can be used instead of the existing type throughout the program.

Type alias do not create new types. They simply provide a new name to an existing type.

The main purpose of type alias is to make our code more readable, and clearer in context for human understanding.

83. What is a set?

Sets is simply a container that can hold multiple value of data type in an unordered list and ensures unique element in the container (i.e. each data appears only once).

Values stored in a set must be hashable. This means it must provide a hashValue property. This is important because sets are unordered, and it uses hashValue is used to access the elements of the sets.

84. What is the main advantages of using set over array ?

The main advantage of using Sets over arrays is when you need to ensure that an item only appears once and when the order of items is not important.

85. How to declare a set in Swift?

You can create an empty set by specifying the type as Set followed by the type of Data it can store within < >.

Example 1: Declaring an empty set

let emptyIntSet:Set = []

print(emptyIntSet)

OR

let emptyIntSet:Set = Set()

print(emptyIntSet)

When you run the program, the output will be:

[ ]

86. How to access set elements in Swift?

You cannot access elements of a set using subscript syntax as arrays. This is because sets are unordered and do not have indices to access the elements.

So, you need to access the set using its methods and properties or using for-in loops.

87. How to add new element in a set?

You can add a new element to a set using insert() method in Swift.

88. What is swift expressions?

An expression is a combination of values, constants, variables, operators, and functions that produces another value. To be simpler, an expression is any valid code that returns a value.

The resulting value is usually one of Swift Data Types e.g. integer, string, and float or more complex data type as functions.

89. Name various types of ranges in Swift?

Types of ranges in swift are

- Closed Range
- Half open Range
- One sided Range

90. Explain Closed Range?

Ranges created using the closed range operator are called as closed range. It includes all the values from lowerbound to upperbound.

Example 1: Printing closed range values using for-in loop

// 1...10 Defines a range containing values 1, 2, 3 up to 10.

for value in 1...10 {

print(value)

}

When you run the program, the output will be:

1

2

3

.

10

91. Explain Half Open Range?

Ranges created using the half open range operator are called as half open ranges. It includes all values from lower bound to upper bound but excludes the upper bound value.

Example : Printing half open range values using for-in loop

// 1..<3 Defines a range containing values 1,2

for value in 1..<3 {

        print(value)

}

When you run the program, the output will be:

1

2

In the above example, we've used for-in loop to see how half-open range works.

Instead of printing all the values, we can clearly see using half open operator only prints 1 and 2, and it excludes the upper bound value (i.e. 3).

92. Explain one sided range?

One sided range are those types of range that continue as far as possible in one direction. It can be created using both half open range operator and closed range operator, but the operator can have a value on only one side.

93. *What do you mean by the term "defer"?*

The term "defer" is a keyword that provides a block of code that executes when the execution is leaving the current scope.

94. *What is a protocol, how do you define your own and when is it used?*

A protocol is like an interface from Java. It defines a list of required and optional methods that a class must/can implement if it adopts the protocol. A common use case is providing a DataSource for UITableView or UICollectionView.

95. *What is function overloading?*

The process we just described is known as function overloading. The process of creating two or more than two functions with the same name but having different number or types of parameters passed is known as function overloading.

96. *How to assign value to a variable in Swift?*

You can assign the value in a variable using the assignment operator (=).

Example : Declaring and assigning a value to a variable

var siteName:String

siteName = "swiftprogramming.com"

print(siteName)

OR

You can also assign the value inline as

var siteName:String = "swiftprogramming.com"

print(siteName)

When you run the program, the output will be:

swiftprogramming.com

97. Explain CodingKey Protocol

The CodingKey enum (Protocol) lets you rename specific properties in case the serialized format doesn't match the requirements of the API. CodingKeys should have nested enum.

98. What is Operator precedence in swift?

Operator precedence is a collection of rules used to evaluate a given mathematical expression. When there are several operators used in a single expression, each part is evaluated in a certain order called as operator precedence. Certain operators have higher priority than others which affects how an expression is evaluated.

99. What is the difference Filter and Map Function ?

Map, we pass in a function that returns a value for each element in an array. The return value of this function represents what an element becomes in our new array.

Filter, we pass in a function that returns either true or false for each element. If the function that we pass returns true for a given element, then the element is included in the final array.

100. What is closure in swift programming?

Swift functions are created using func keyword. However, there is another special type of function in Swift, known as closures that can be defined without using keyword func and a function name.

Like functions, closures can accept parameters and return values. It also contains a set of statements which executes after you call it and can be assigned to a variable/constant as functions.

101. Why Closures are used?

Closures are mainly used for two reasons:

Completion blocks

Closures help you to be notified when some task has finished its execution. See Closure as a completion handler to learn more about it.

Higher order functions

Closures can be passed as an input parameter for higher order functions. A higher order function is just a type of function that accepts function as an input and returns value of type function as output.

For this purpose, it's better to use closures in replacement of function because closure omits the func keyword and function name that makes the code more readable and shorter.

102. What is trailing closure in Swift?

If a function accepts a closure as its last parameter, the closure can be passed like a function body between { }. This type of closure written outside of function call parentheses is known as trailing closure.

103. What is an auto closure in swift?

A closure which is marked with @autoclosure keyword is known as autoclosure. @autoclosure keyword creates an automatic closure around the expression by adding a {}. Therefore, you can omit braces {} when passing closures to a function.

104. Why auto closure is used?

The main advantage of using autoclosure is that you don't need to wrap the expression in curly braces {} when calling closures.

105. Are closures value or reference types?

Closures are reference types. If a closure is assigned to a variable and the variable is copied into another variable, a reference to the same closure and its capture list is also copied.

106.Can you describe a situation where you might get a circular reference in Swift, and how you'd solve it?

A circular reference happens when two instances hold a strong reference to each other, causing a memory leak because none of two instances will ever be deallocated. The reason is that an instance cannot be deallocated if there's a strong reference to it, but each instance keeps the other alive because of its strong reference.

You'd solve the problem by breaking the strong circular reference by replacing one of the strong references with a weak or an unowned reference.

Please check out other bestselling books of this author

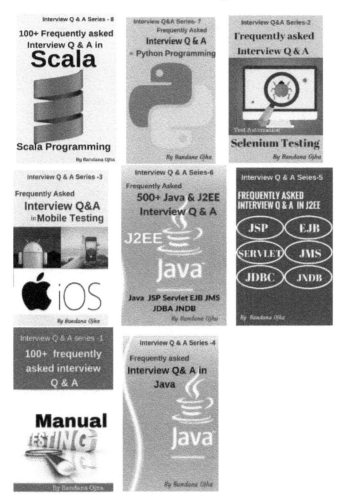